| DATE DUE | | |
|---|---|---|
| OC 03 '02 | | |
| OC 24 '02 | | |
| MY 12 '03 | | |
| MR 10 '04 | | |
| OC 16 '06 | | |
| MR 30 '07 | | |
| MAR 0 5 '08 | | |
| MAR 2 5 '08 | | |
| MAR 0 2 '11 | | |
| | | |
| | | |
| | | |

# THE AMERICAN REVOLUTION

## "Give Me Liberty, or Give Me Death!"

Deborah Kent

—American War Series—

**Enslow Publishers, Inc.**

40 Industrial Road        PO Box 38
Box 398             Aldershot
Berkeley Heights, NJ 07922   Hants GU12 6BP
USA                 UK

http://www.enslow.com

> *"I know not what course others may take; but as for me,*
> *give me liberty, or give me death!"*
> —Patrick Henry, March 3, 1775.

Copyright 1994 © by Deborah Kent

**Library of Congress Cataloging-in-Publication Data**

Kent, Deborah.
   The American Revolution: "Give me liberty, or give me death" / Deborah Kent.
       p.   cm. — (American war series)
   Includes bibliographical references (p. ) and index.
   ISBN 0-89490-521-X
   1. United States—History—Revolution, 1775-1783—Juvenile literature. [1. United States—History—Revolution, 1775-1783.] I. Series.
   E208.K46   1993
   973.3—dc20                                    93-39046
                                                    CIP
                                                    AC
Printed in the United States of America

10  9  8  7  6

**Index Credit:** Ann Heinrichs

**Illustration Credits:** Courtesy of the Prints and Photographs Division, Library of Congress, pp. 20, 29, 35, 42, 54, 69, 70, 89; Enslow Publishers, Inc., pp. 13, 25; National Archives, pp. 8, 9, 11, 15, 17, 30, 33, 39, 43, 48, 50, 52, 56, 61, 72, 77, 79, 81, 84, 86, 91, 94, 99, 103, 107, 109, 112, 116.

**Cover Illustration:** Courtesy of the Prints and Photographs Division, Library of Congress.

# Contents

*Foreword*

Growing up in New Jersey, I always felt that the American Revolution had taken place close to home. Washington crossed the Delaware River to win a battle at Trenton, our own state capital. He and his troops spent a cruel winter in Morristown. On a sweltering day in June a woman called Molly Pitcher carried water for the Americans during the Battle of Monmouth. And only three miles from my house in Little Falls, I could walk along Riflecamp Road, named in honor of the patriot troops who once pitched their tents in the nearby woods. The American Revolution seemed like a glorious era—when people fought for the cause of freedom. Of course many died—but they died the noble deaths of heroes.

I was shocked one day when my father declared that, if he had lived back in 1776, he would have been a Tory. I knew about the Tories, those colonists who had stubbornly remained loyal to the British throughout the war. They were turncoats, traitors—or were they?

Every question has two sides, or more. Like the rebellious colonists, the British soldiers and American Loyalists believed they fought for a cause that was honorable and just. Both sides had their moments of valor, and on occasion both committed appalling atrocities. In every battle, men on both sides suffered and died. No ideals, however noble, softened the pain inflicted by musket balls and slashing bayonets.

Like most wars, the American Revolution could not be contained once it had begun. It swelled into a major conflict that spanned six long, bloody years. It stretched beyond the thirteen rebelling colonies to reach the American frontier and even the West Indies. Other countries—France, Spain, and Holland—were eventually swept into the fighting.

It must have been hard to remember ideals as battle casualties mounted and smallpox and other diseases ravaged the camps. Yet in the end, after the last roar of the cannon faded, a new nation emerged—one rooted in the ideals of democracy, a belief in government for the people, by the people. Over the last two centuries, the democratic principles that the American Revolution set in motion still echo around the world. These ideals, which shook the lives of thousands of men and women more than 200 years ago, are indeed still very close to home.

*What a glorious morning for America!*
—Samuel Adams, on hearing gunfire at Lexington,
April 19, 1775.

# 1 The Shot Heard Round the World

 The British were taking no chances. The officers shook the men awake instead of rousing them with the usual shouts and bugle calls. There was no talking as the troops assembled in the darkness on Boston Common. The march got underway. When the men reached a brook, they waded across—the stamping of army boots on the hollow planks of the wooden bridge would have alerted people in the neighboring farmhouses. General Thomas Gage had instructed his troops to move with the utmost secrecy. He wanted them to take the villages of Lexington and Concord completely by surprise.

Gage had learned that Samuel Adams and John Hancock, two ringleaders in the growing unrest among

Remembered for his fiery speeches, Samuel Adams was one of the first American colonists to call for independence from Great Britain.

A prominent Boston businessman, John Hancock was a vocal patriot in 1775. A year later, he signed the Declaration of Independence with bold, sweeping strokes that won him lasting fame.

the American colonists, were staying at a house in Lexington. As long as they were at liberty, Gage feared that peace could never be restored. Gage ordered his men to capture the two troublemakers. Then they were to march on to Concord and seize American stores of guns and ammunition. If all went well, the rebellion could be put down in a single night's work.

For more than ten years, tension had been mounting between Great Britain and its thirteen American colonies. The city of Boston had become the hub of American protest against British control. By April 18, 1775, when Gage's troops set out for Lexington, Boston was a city under siege. British soldiers patrolled the streets, and British warships blockaded the harbor. Most Bostonians resented the outsiders, and some were determined to fight back.

Every night that spring, colonial spies observed the comings and goings of the British troops and listened hungrily to every scrap of conversation. Even before the troops mustered on Boston Common, the Americans knew what Gage planned to do. Two messengers on horseback galloped toward Lexington with the news. Their names were William Dawes and Paul Revere.

Both Dawes and Revere rode at top speed, warning everyone along the way that the British were coming. Today most Americans know about Paul Revere's ride, but few recognize Dawes' name. Henry Wadsworth Longfellow immortalized Revere in a famous poem which begins, "Listen, my children, and you shall hear / Of the midnight ride of Paul Revere . . ." Because the

On the night of April 18, 1775, Paul Revere rode 18 miles from Boston to Lexington, warning the Massachusetts colonists that British soldiers were coming.

name *Revere* rhymes more easily than the name *Dawes*, one man became a legend, while the other was nearly forgotten.

Eight colonial guards surrounded the house where Hancock and Adams slept. "About midnight, Colonel Paul Revere rode up and requested admittance," Sergeant William Munroe wrote later. "I told him the family had just retired, and had requested that they might not be disturbed by any noise about the house. 'Noise!' he said. 'You'll have noise enough before long! The Regulars are coming out!' We then permitted him to pass."[1] With the advance warning, Hancock and Adams had plenty of time to slip away. Captain John Parker alerted his company of Lexington militiamen and gathered them on the village green.

In the meantime, the British got off to a slow start. They left Boston at 10 P.M., crossing the Charles River into Cambridge. There they waited more than two hours for provisions to arrive. At last, at 2 A.M., they began the 18-mile march to Lexington.

The first streaks of dawn lit the sky when the British regular troops, led by Colonel Francis Smith, marched into Lexington. By now the militiamen had grown tired of waiting for something to happen, and most of them had adjourned to the nearby tavern. When the drum sounded for them to reassemble, they scrambled about in confusion. Some panicked and fled. Others realized they had no ammunition, and rushed to the town meeting-house where it was stored. At last Parker gathered some 70 men on the green to meet the enemy.

# Concord and Lexington

AMERICAN ADVANCE TO INTERCEPT BRITISH

Concord R.

North Bridge

Liberty Pole

Merriam's Corner

Lexington Rd.

Cemetery

LEXINGTON

Buckman Tavern

outh ridge

CONCORD

Munroe Tavern

BOSTON (5 mi)

Emerson House

Church

Burying Ground

ROUTE OF PAUL REVERE
AND OF BRITISH TROOPS ADVANCING
FROM BOSTON ON LEXINGTON AND CONCORD

EXINGTON AND CONCORD ARE DRAWN IN A LARGER SCALE THAN BOSTON.

# Boston

MEDFORD

Malden River

Mystic River

LEXINGTON (5 miles)
CONCORD (11 miles)

SWAMP LAND

NODDLES ISLAND

Bunker Hill

Breed's Hill

Harvard College

CAMBRIDGE

Charleston

Beacon Hill

Commons

Charles River

Boston Harbor

BOSTON

Site of
Boston Tea Party

ROXBURY

DORCHESTER HTS.

Map showing the route from Boston to the battlegrounds at
Lexington and Concord.

The British troops were an imposing sight: six companies advancing in orderly rows in their scarlet coats, muskets and bayonets ready. "Don't fire unless fired upon," Parker told his men. "But if they want a war, let it begin here."

To this day, no one knows who fired the first shot. One militiaman described what happened: "The commanding officer advanced within a few yards of us and exclaimed, 'Disperse, you damned rebels! You dogs, run! Rush on, my boys!' and fired his pistol."[2] But Col. Smith, the British commander, gave a different version. "They in confusion went off, . . . only one of them fired before he went, and three or four more jumped over a wall and fired from behind it among the soldiers."[3] Within moments, guns blazed on both sides. When the militiamen scattered, eight Americans lay dead on Lexington Green. The British fired a triumphant volley into the air and gave three cheers.

From Lexington, the British marched six miles further to Concord. But William Dawes and another messenger, Dr. Samuel Prescot, had gotten there before them. (Paul Revere was captured by British soldiers soon after he left Lexington.) The colonists had time to hide most of the weapons and powder that the British hoped to seize. British troops and Americans again exchanged fire on Concord Bridge, and the British were forced to withdraw. Two men on each side were killed.

Now the British began the long march back to Boston. "The country was an amazing strong one, full of hills, woods, stone walls, etc., which the rebels did not

In the first military confrontation of the American Revolution, colonial militiamen and redcoated British soldiers clashed on Lexington Green.

fail to take advantage of," one British officer wrote. "They were all lined with people who kept an incessant fire upon us. . . . They were so concealed there was hardly any seeing them. In this way we marched between nine and ten miles, their numbers increasing from all parts, while ours were reduced by deaths, wounds, and fatigue; and we were totally surrounded with such an incessant fire as it is impossible to conceive."[4] At times the British and Americans fought hand to hand with bayonets, clubs, and hatchets. British soldiers looted farmhouses and set them on fire.

In Lexington the British had cheered their victory. But they failed to capture either John Hancock or Samuel Adams, or the arms stored in Concord. Worse still, they left a tragic trail of dead and wounded men on their tortured journey back to Boston.

Many Americans hailed the day as a triumph for the colonists. Ill-trained and poorly armed though they were, the Americans had shown their fierce fighting spirit. They were a force to be reckoned with.

Yet some colonists took a more sober view. John Adams, a distant cousin of the fiery Samuel Adams, described his feelings in a letter: "Yesterday produced a scene the most shocking New England ever beheld. . . . When I reflect and consider that the fight was between those whose parents but a few generations ago were brothers, I shudder at the thought; and there is no knowing where our calamities will end."[5]

More than 50 years later, the philosopher and writer Ralph Waldo Emerson commemorated the crucial events

John Adams was a leader in the Continental Congress. He became the second president of the United States. This is a copy of a portrait by Rembrandt Peale.

of April 19, 1775, in his "Concord Hymn." Emerson is somewhat misleading—the first shots were fired at Lexington, not at Concord—but he understood the significance of the conflict that began on that fateful day. He wrote:

> By the rude bridge that arched the flood,
> Their flag by April's breeze unfurled,
> Here once the embattled farmers stood,
> And fired the shot heard round the world.

*Is life so dear or peace so sweet as to be purchased*
*at the price of chains and slavery?*
*Forbid it, Almighty God. I know not what*
*course others may take, but as for me,*
*give me liberty or give me death!*
—Patrick Henry, March 23, 1775

# 2 Taxation Without Representation

 Wherever people gathered throughout the colonies—in the taverns, at the market, on the Common—there were grumblings of discontent. What gave those men in London the right to tax the colonists? In Massachusetts, self-respecting Bostonians questioned if they should tolerate such treatment.

## The Stamp Act

The trouble began early in 1765, when Parliament in London levied a new tax on Britain's 13 colonies. The tax took the form of an official stamp or seal that the colonists would have to purchase each time they drew up a legal document, such as a will or a deed of property. Stamps would also be required with the purchase of such

Under the Stamp Act of 1765, a special stamp had to be purchased with most legal documents drawn up in the colonies

everyday items as glass, paint, paper, and even playing cards.

People in England were well used to taxes. Between 1756 and 1763, England was involved in a long and costly conflict called the Seven Years' War (becoming the French and Indian War in North America). To finance that struggle, new taxes were levied each year—on tobacco, beer, sugar, newspapers, and linen. But the British people elected representatives to speak for them in Parliament. The Americans, however, had no voting representative to argue on their behalf. The Stamp Act seemed a grave injustice.

In May, 1765, a handsome young lawyer named Patrick Henry spoke before the Virginia Assembly, or House of Burgesses. He stated that the colonists in America had the same rights as all other British citizens. Therefore, they could not be taxed unless they were represented in Parliament. Henry's arguments formed the basis of the Virginia Resolves, a document which, although not passed by the Burgesses, helped people in several of the other colonies take a similar stand.

Nowhere was resistance against the Stamp Act stronger than in Massachusetts. In Boston, young men calling themselves the Sons of Liberty stirred the citizens to protest. Some resistance was peaceful. Many people chose not to buy paint or glass rather than pay for the hated stamps. But as the months passed, the protest became more violent. Supplies of stamps were seized and destroyed. Stamp distributors were forced to resign.

Finally, late in August of 1765, Boston erupted in a series of riots.

Toward evening on August 26, a mob looted the homes of several officials thought to sympathize with Parliament and the British King. Hardest hit was Lieutenant Governor Thomas Hutchinson. In a letter, Governor Francis Bernard described what happened:

> [Hutchinson] was at supper with his family when he received advice that the mob were coming to him. He immediately sent away his children and determined to stay in the house himself, but happily his eldest daughter turned and declared she would not stir from the house unless he went with her; by which means she got him away, which was undoubtedly the occasion for saving his life. . . . Everything movable was destroyed in the most minute manner except such things of value as were worth carrying off. . . . The loss to be most lamented is . . . a large and valuable collection of manuscripts and original papers which he had been gathering all his lifetime. . . . The loss to the public is as irretrievable as it is to himself.[1]

In its fury, the mob tried to tear the house to the ground, but it was too solidly built. At daybreak its brick walls still stood, ravaged and forlorn.

Few members of Parliament had imagined the Stamp Act would arouse such a tempest. Perhaps the law had been a serious mistake. In 1766, the Stamp Act was repealed. The colonists greeted the news with fireworks and a clamor of church bells. But the trouble had only begun.

## A Question of Power

For more than 150 years, men, women, and children from England had been settling in the New World. By 1765, a chain of 13 colonies stretched along the eastern coast of North America from New Hampshire to Georgia. In addition to people of English descent, many others lived in the colonies. About one-third of the people in Pennsylvania were German. Dutch, Swedish, and Finnish settlers lived in New Jersey and Delaware. Scotch-Irish immigrants (people of Scottish heritage who had lived for a few generations in Ireland) settled further west, along the American frontier. About 17 percent of the people of the colonies were of African descent. Slavery was firmly entrenched in the south, and even in New England it was an accepted part of life.

Most of the colonists were farmers, though Boston, New York, Philadelphia, and Charleston, South Carolina, were thriving seaports. During the 1700's, the population of the colonies increased tenfold—from 250,000 in 1700 to nearly 2.5 million in 1775. By today's standards, this population seems sparse. As many people as live in present-day Chicago were scattered along the fringe of a vast continent. But the colonies were flourishing. England, the mother country, seemed far away across the stormy Atlantic.

Until the controversy over the Stamp Act, few colonists questioned their ties with Great Britain. England was the source of manufactured goods such as linen, paper, and glass. It provided arms and soldiers to defend the colonies against Indian uprisings. The Crown appointed royal governors and many other officials, but the colonists elected their own governing assemblies. In general, England left the colonies relatively free to handle their own affairs.

This freedom was suddenly challenged by the passage of the Stamp Act. For the first time, many colonists began to wonder about their relationship with England. If Parliament had the right to pass laws affecting the colonies, then the colonies should be represented in Parliament.

King George III and most members of Parliament had other ideas. If England was the mother country, then the colonies were her children. In the 1700's, children did not question their parents' authority. If they were rebellious, they should be and were punished.

In 1767, Parliament passed a new set of laws known as the Townshend Acts. The Townshend Acts imposed taxes on glass, paint, lead, tea, and a variety of other goods that the colonies imported. Once more, the colonists were outraged. The cry, "Taxation without representation is tyranny!" resounded from New England to Charleston. In Massachusetts, Samuel Adams wrote a letter of protest, calling on the colonies to launch a united resistance. Without Governor Bernard's consent, the Massachusetts Assembly approved Adams' letter. The assemblies of New Hampshire,

# The Thirteen Colonies

Quebec

Montreal

St. Lawrence R.

Lake Superior

Lake Champlain

Lake Ontario

**MAINE**
(part of MA)

**NH**

② ⑩ ⑦

⑥

**NY**

**MA**
**CT**

① ③

Boston

**RI**

Lake Huron

Lake Michigan

Lake Erie

**PA**

④ ⑫

Long Island (NY)

⑨ ⑪

Philadelphia

⑤

New York

⑧

**NJ**

**DE**

**MD**

Ohio River

Vincennes

**VA**

⑰

⑮

**NC**

⑭ ⑬

⑯ **SC**

**GA**

Charleston

Mississippi River

Savannah

*Atlantic
Ocean*

*Gulf of Mexico*

**FL**
(Spain)

**Key to Battles:**

① Lexington and Concord
② Fort Ticonderoga
③ Bunker (Breed's) Hill
④ White Plains
⑤ Trenton
⑥ Oriskany
⑦ Bennington
⑧ Brandywine
⑨ Germantown

⑩ Saratoga
⑪ Princeton
⑫ Monmouth
⑬ Kings Mtn.
⑭ Cowpens
⑮ Guilford Court House
⑯ Camden
⑰ Yorktown

Territory gained by the United States
in the Treaty of Paris 1783.

- - - - - - Represents uncertain or
disputed boundaries

Map of the thirteen British colonies which fought for independence
in the American Revolution. Major battle sites of the war are shown.

New Jersey, and Connecticut supported Massachusetts' stand. Virginia drafted a similar letter of its own.

As an even stronger measure, Massachusetts and New York announced a boycott of British goods. Philadelphia soon followed their example, as did Charleston and other southern ports.

Throughout the colonies, women gave up serving tea and wearing imported clothes. They took a new pride in weaving and wearing homespun cloth, even though it was rough and scratchy to the skin. But plenty of British goods still found their way into the colonies. Some merchants refused to co-operate with the boycott. Others avoided paying the import duties by smuggling. Late at night, boats with their oars muffled, delivered wine, molasses, tea, and other goods in quiet coves and along hidden creeks, beyond the reach of any customshouse official.

In London, Parliament and the King concluded that radicals in Boston were stirring up all the trouble. By punishing Boston, they could set an example for all of the colonies, and bring them to order again.

In 1768, a fleet of British warships sailed into Boston Harbor. The citizens of the town watched in amazement as companies of redcoated soldiers disembarked, their bayonets gleaming in the sunlight. To the music of fifes and drums they marched through the once quiet streets. Their very presence seemed a threat and a warning.

General Thomas Gage was in command of the Boston troops. He saw the Bostonians as "mutinous desperadoes . . . guilty of sedition."[2] The British soldiers were marching into enemy territory to stamp out the rebellion.

## A Massacre and a Tea Party

Moonlight shone on the snowy street as Private White stood on watch. As a British soldier, he had grown used to taunts from American rowdies. But on the night of March 5, 1770, one young apprentice went too far. When he insulted an officer standing nearby, White smacked the boy on the ear.

Over the past year and a half, the people of Boston had come to resent the British troops whose tents dotted the Common. Often they were noisy and drunk. Sometimes the soldiers stopped people on the streets, demanding to know who they were and where they were going. Peaceful citizens felt like strangers in their own city.

Minutes after Private White struck the apprentice, an angry crowd gathered. Men and boys hurled snowballs and chunks of ice at the sentry, who retreated to the doorway of the customshouse. He shouted for help, and eight soldiers hurried to his aid. Behind them came Captain Thomas Preston, the officer in command.

A church bell tolled, usually a signal of fire, and more colonists rushed into the streets. Some brought buckets of water, ready to put out a blaze. Others carried clubs and muskets, prepared for trouble of a different kind.

One of the people who hurried toward the commotion was Crispus Attucks, a tall, stocky African American from the nearby town of Framingham. Weeks later, a slave named Andrew testified that Attucks raised a stick and tried to hit a British officer. "[He] then turned around and struck the grenadier's gun . . . and immediately fell in with his club and knocked his gun away, and struck him over the head," Andrew stated. "[He] held the bayonet with his left hand, and twitched it, and cried, 'Kill the dogs! Knock them down!' This was the general cry. The people then crowded in."[3]

The crowd pressed around the soldiers who were trying to rescue White, holding them captive as well. Captain Preston ordered his men to load their muskets. When someone knocked a soldier to the ground, the soldier came up shooting. Suddenly gunfire peppered the crowd. Three Americans were killed, and two more died later of their wounds. The first to fall in the assault was Crispus Attucks.

Words of the killings swept through the city. People poured into the streets, grieving and appalled. True, the Americans had taunted the soldiers, had even threatened them with sticks. But the soldiers turned on them with musket fire. The deadly confrontation was remembered ever after as the Boston Massacre.

Over the next few years, Parliament repealed nearly all of the Townshend Acts. But to show that the colonists were still subject to British control, one tax was left in place—a duty on the importation of tea. In the spring of 1773, a new law reduced the tax of tea sold by the British East India Company, thus giving the company a virtual monopoly. Tea had long been a favorite beverage

Killed during the Boston Massacre, Crispus Attucks is remembered as one of the first Americans to die in the struggle for independence.

On March 5, 1770 British soldiers fired on a crowd of angry protestors in a Boston street. Five Americans died—the first casualties of the struggle for independence.

in colonial homes. Now, as John Adams' wife Abigail put it, tea became "the weed of slavery."

Up and down the American coast, people protested the importation of British tea. In Charleston, it was left in warehouses to rot. In Philadelphia and New York, officials forbade ships from landing tea at all.

When three ships loaded with tea anchored in Boston Harbor, Thomas Hutchinson (now governor of Massachusetts) insisted that the cargo should be unloaded and sold. At two mass meetings, Boston citizens demanded that the tea be sent back to England. But Hutchinson refused to comply.

On the night of December 16, 1773, a band of patriots gathered at Griffin's Wharf, where the three merchant ships had docked. They planned a peaceful protest, which has come to be known as the Boston Tea Party. In an attempt to remain anonymous, they disguised themselves as Indians. They darkened their faces and hands with coal dust, wrapped blankets around their shoulders, and carried clubs and hatchets.

One participant in the tea party, George Hughes, later described the experience:

> We were ordered to board all the ships at the same time, which we promptly obeyed. . . . We then were ordered by our commander to open the hatches and take out all the chests of tea and throw them overboard, and we immediately proceeded to execute his orders, first cutting and splitting the chests with our tomahawks so as thoroughly to expose them to the effects of the water. In about three hours from the time we

went on board we had thus broken and thrown overboard every tea chest to be found in the ship. . . . No disorder took place during that transaction, and it was observed at that time that the stillest night ensued that Boston had enjoyed for many months.[4]

No one was hurt during the Boston Tea Party, and except for the 342 tea chests that were dumped into the harbor, almost no property was damaged. Yet once again the people of Boston had made an emphatic statement to Parliament. They were not obedient children. They were men and women with clear ideas about their rights, and they were determined to be heard.

## The War Begins

The unrest in the colonies sparked spirited debate in Great Britain. British conservatives argued that the colonies had been established to enrich the mother country and served no other purpose. The outspoken essayist Samuel Johnson wrote that if the colonists wanted representation in Parliament, they should move to England. But the economist Adam Smith warned that England might lose its colonies altogether if they were not given their rights.

News of the Boston Tea Party swung King George III and a majority in Parliament strongly against the colonies. The Americans, and especially the people of Massachusetts, had overstepped their limits. They must be punished. In the spring of 1774, Parliament passed a series of new laws, known in America as the Intolerable Acts. The Intolerable Acts were aimed particularly at

On the night of December 16, 1773, a band of colonists disguised as Indians threw 342 chests of tea into Boston Harbor to protest British import duties.

Massachusetts. One law closed the port of Boston to all trade. Another replaced Massachusetts' elected assembly with a body appointed by the Crown. The Quartering Act affected all of the colonies. It required that British troops be housed in public buildings and private homes.

The new laws went into effect on June 1, 1774. Boston observed the occasion with a day of fasting and prayer. Church bells tolled somberly, and public buildings were draped in black crepe. British warships blockaded Boston Harbor, and troops poured into the city.

Since their founding, the American colonies had been distinctly separate entities. They communicated more with England than with each other. But the Intolerable Acts awakened a new spirit of unity. What happened to Boston could easily happen to New York or Philadelphia. The other colonies rallied to Boston's support. From as far away as the Carolinas, supplies of food reached the beleaguered city. Now sharing a common enemy, the colonies drew together.

In September 1774, twelve colonies sent delegates to join Pennsylvania's delegates in Philadelphia for the First Continental Congress. Only Georgia was not represented. Some of the ablest men in the colonies attended this congress. Among them were Thomas Jefferson and George Washington of Virginia, Caesar Rodney of Delaware, John Dickinson of Pennsylvania, and Samuel and John Adams of Massachusetts.

Even at this point, few of the delegates really wanted the colonies to sever their connection with England.

Delegates from twelve of the thirteen colonies met in Philadelphia at the First Continental Congress in 1774.

Most hoped that they could reach a compromise with Parliament and the King. But after seven weeks of debate, they agreed to break off all trade with Great Britain. Committees of Safety would be set up throughout the colonies to enforce the boycott. For the first time, the colonies combined their strength to act as one.

In Massachusetts, tension mounted steadily. By November 1774, 11 British regiments were quartered in Boston. Thousands of people fled the colony, but others chose to stay and resist. In nearly every village, farmers and tradesmen formed bands of militia, practicing maneuvers on the public squares. A supply of muskets and gunpowder was concealed in the town of Concord. Massachusetts was under siege, and it was preparing for war.

It was only a short step from preparation to war itself. The Americans and the British took that step on April 19, 1775, when they faced one another at Lexington and Concord.

*These are the times that try men's souls.*
*The summer soldier and the sunshine patriot*
*will, in this crisis, shrink from the service of*
*their country; but he that stands it now, deserves*
*the love and thanks of man and woman.*
—Thomas Paine, *The American Crisis*, December 1776.

# 3 Fighting for Independence

 Outrage swept the colonies with the news of the events at Lexington and Concord. From as far away as Georgia, supplies of food reached occupied Boston. New Hampshire and Connecticut sent soldiers to support the beleaguered city. But the American troops who gathered outside Boston had no artillery to bombard the British in their stronghold.

## The Great Jehovah and the Continental Congress

Though they had a common enemy, the colonies continued to function as separate entities, however. Soon after the Battle of Lexington, the Connecticut Committee of Safety sent Ethan Allen of Vermont to seize Ticonderoga, a British fort on Lake Champlain, New York. At almost the same time Benedict Arnold, a druggist from New Haven, persuaded the Committee of Safety in Massachusetts to let him launch his own Ticonderoga campaign. Early in May of 1775, Allen and Arnold met two miles below Ticonderoga—Arnold with no troops, Allen with 200 of his "Green Mountain Boys." After a fierce quarrel over the command of the expedition, they agreed to work together, with Arnold serving mainly as an observer.

Fort Ticonderoga had fallen on hard times. Though it was well supplied with cannons and ammunition, it was manned by only two officers and 48 soldiers. At dawn on May 10, Arnold and Allen took the fort completely by surprise. Not a shot was fired. Allen bounded up the stairs to the officers' quarters. "The captain came immediately to the door with his britches in his hand," Allen wrote later. "When I ordered him to deliver to me the fort instantly, he asked me by whose authority I demanded it. I answered, 'In the name of the great Jehovah and the Continental Congress.'"[1]

With barely a protest, the captain turned over the fort to the Americans. Two days later, Ethan Allen captured the nearby fort at Crown Point, again with little British resistance. The Americans now held a strategic base at the entrance to Lake George. Furthermore, they had seized 16 howitzers and 45 cannon, heavy weapons that would be invaluable to the American war effort.

Without a struggle, Captain de la Place surrendered Fort
Ticonderoga to Ethan Allen in May, 1775.

## Bloodshed on Breed's Hill

The British still held Boston, but rebel lines nearly surrounded the city. Although the British still controlled the seas, they were unable to make a move on land. Gage and his troops were virtual prisoners. In early June 1775, three more British generals arrived to take charge. None of the three—William Howe, John Burgoyne, and Henry Clinton—had an outstanding military record. Furthermore, they were all bitterly jealous of one another. British Prime Minister Lord North once remarked, "I know not what the Americans will think of them, but I know they make me tremble."[2]

Early in the same June, the Massachusetts Committee of Safety learned that Gage planned to seize Bunker Hill near Charlestown. Bunker Hill was a strategic position overlooking Boston. The Americans determined to fortify the hill before Gage had a chance to capture it himself. On the night of June 16, 1,600 Americans moved quietly down the Charlestown Peninsula, half a mile from Boston across the Charles River. At the last minute their leaders decided to fortify Breed's Hill instead of Bunker Hill. Breed's Hill was slightly closer to Boston.

The air hung hot and stifling, but there was no rest for the Americans on Breed's Hill. With picks and shovels they dug deep trenches, outlining a great rectangular fort, or redoubt, 130 feet in length. Within the trenches they built six-foot-high walls made of bundles of sticks and hay reinforced with earth. One of the diggers, Peter

Brown, later recalled, "We worked there undiscovered until about five in the morning, and then we saw our danger, being against eight ships of the line and all Boston fortified against us. The danger we were in made us think there was treachery, and that we were brought there to be all slain."[3]

At first light, the British were amazed to see earthen walls across the river. At once the warships in the harbor opened fire. The ships' guns did little damage, but the noise was terrifying. "We began to be almost beat out," Peter Brown wrote, "being tired by our labor having no sleep the night before, and no victuals, and no drink but rum."[4]

The following afternoon, barges ferried 2,200 British troops to the peninsula. Commanded by newly arrived General William Howe, the soldiers attempted to march toward the redoubt in close-packed, orderly lines. They wore thick winter uniforms despite the June heat, and staggered beneath packs loaded with blankets and food. Mud sucked at their heavy boots.

As the British grenadiers approached the hill, the Americans suddenly hailed them with musket fire. For Howe it was "a moment that I never felt before, a moment of horror."

The Americans repelled two British attacks. But eventually they ran out of ammunition, and reinforcements never arrived. British troops swarmed over the walls into the redoubt. Most of the Americans managed to escape, but about 30 men were trapped inside. Mercilessly, British bayonets slashed them to pieces.

British ships bombard American fortifications on Breed's Hill overlooking Charlestown, Massachusetts.

On June 17, 1775, British and American troops fought fiercely for Breed's Hill and Bunker Hill on the Charlestown Peninsula overlooking Boston.

By nightfall the town of Charlestown lay in ashes, and the British controlled the entire peninsula. But after the long, bloody battle, British casualties were even heavier than those of the Americans. A wounded British colonel remarked, "A few such victories would ruin the army."[5]

## Washington Takes Command

In the spring of 1775, the Continental Congress met once more in Philadelphia. The first order of business was the creation of an army to fight for the American cause. John Hancock, who had avoided capture in Lexington, served as president of the Continental Congress. Though he was a businessman without military experience, he believed he should command the new army. Much to his chagrin, however, Congress appointed a Virginia planter named George Washington on June 15, 1775.

As a young man Washington had fought for the British in the French and Indian War. He had been made a colonel when he was only 22. He was tall and sturdy, and carried himself with an air of dignity, though his smile was marred by decaying teeth. Washington was as modest as Hancock was arrogant. He warned the Congress that he was unequal to the task before him, and he refused to accept a monthly salary. In a letter to his wife Martha he wrote, "I should enjoy more real happiness in one month with you at home than I have the most distant prospect of finding abroad if my stay were to be seven times seven years."

On July 2, Washington took charge of the American forces in Cambridge, across the Charles River from Boston. He found 14,000 men who knew almost nothing of military discipline. Guards wandered away from their posts, or chatted with the enemy. Men and officers were on a first-name basis. Officers were reluctant to give orders, and the men were unwilling to obey. The men only enlisted for a few months at a time, and most enlistments would soon run out.

The camps in Cambridge were noisy, chaotic, and filthy. Yet one visitor found much to admire:

> Every tent is a portraiture of the temper and tastes of the persons that encamp in it. Some are made of boards, some of sailcloth, . . . Others are made of stone and turf, and others again of birch and other brush. . . . [Some] are curiously wrought with doors and windows done with reeds and withes in the manner of a basket. . . . I think that the variety of the American camp is on the whole rather a beauty than a blemish to the army.[6]

At once Washington set about to shape this boisterous collection of individuals into a functioning army. With few reliable officers, he was forced to deal with every aspect of military life himself—from maneuvers and musket practice to rations, bedding, and latrines. He forbade swearing, and ordered the men to attend church services regularly.

Most of the men gathered in Cambridge were young

white farmers. They had enlisted in search of adventure, as well as to fight the British. A few soldiers were slaves of African ancestry. They were sent to serve by their masters, or ran away and enlisted in the hope of winning their freedom. Whatever their background, the soldiers had little sense that they were fighting for the united colonies. Over and over, Washington exhorted them to think of themselves not as New Hampshire men or Rhode Islanders, but as Americans, working together for a common cause.

Encouraged by the success at Ticonderoga, General Washington sent Benedict Arnold and General Richard Montgomery on a daring expedition to Canada in the autumn of 1775. Battling storms, hunger, and smallpox, their men struggled through the northern woods. Montgomery was able to occupy Montreal, and then marched with Arnold toward Quebec. The Americans were defeated at Quebec, and Montgomery was killed. The Canadians were not interested in joining forces with the Americans. Throughout the war, they remained loyal to England.

## The British Evacuate Boston

Early in February 1776, an extraordinary cavalcade reached Cambridge. On huge sledges that creaked and ground over the snow came 45 cannons and 16 howitzers, the pride of Ticonderoga and Crown Point. The mastermind behind this remarkable feat of transport was Colonel Henry Knox, a big, bearlike man who reminded some people of a cannon himself. Knox and his men had maneuvered their unwieldy freight across frozen lakes and rivers, uphill and down, through storms of rain and snow to their final destination.

On the night of March 4, 2,000 Americans soldiers hastily erected two redoubts on Dorchester Heights, an elevation overlooking Boston and its harbor. Defending the Heights were some of the cannon that had made the perilous journey from the north. The British awoke to a new landscape of rebel fortifications. General Howe made up his mind to abandon the city. On March 17 some 10,000 British troops and 1,000 Loyalists left for Halifax in Nova Scotia. Boston was in the hands of the American patriots at last.

## The Final Parting

Bloody battles had raged in Massachusetts. In Virginia the royal governor had tried to stir up a slave rebellion against the colonists and had burned the port of Norfolk. Yet many colonists still hoped for reconciliation with England. Ties were so strong that they could not imagine breaking with the mother country.

In January 1776, a recent English immigrant named Thomas Paine published a slender pamphlet entitled *Common Sense*. In the simplest terms he explained why America should be independent. England was not a nurturing mother, he claimed, but a tyrant from whom the first colonists had fled. A continent could not be governed forever by a tiny island. And every time England went to war, the colonies were dragged into the conflict against their will. "O ye that love mankind!" Paine

A recent immigrant from England, Thomas Paine is best known for his pamphlet *Common Sense*. His writing persuaded many colonists that America should become independent.

wrote. "Ye that dare oppose not only the tyranny but the tyrant, stand forth! . . . O receive the fugitive, and prepare in time an asylum for mankind!" Some 120,000 copies of the pamphlet were sold within three months. Its logic was inescapable, and its words were a call to action.

In the months that followed, North Carolina, Rhode Island, Massachusetts, and Virginia authorized their delegates in Congress to ask for separation from England. New Jersey and Delaware, Maryland and Pennsylvania still wavered. But early in June, Congress appointed a committee to draft a declaration of independence. The committee consisted of five men: John Adams, Benjamin Franklin, Roger Sherman, Robert Livingston, and Thomas Jefferson.

Thomas Jefferson was a lawyer and tobacco planter with a quick, wide-ranging mind. His interests included architecture, music, and government. He was also a talented writer. Drawing on his studies of democracy in ancient Greece, as well as more recent European thought, Jefferson wrote almost the entire first draft of the Declaration of Independence. The rest of the committee suggested a few minor changes, and on June 28, 1776, the Congress saw the completed document.

The Declaration of Independence sparked fierce debate among the delegates to the Congress. To declare independence from Great Britain was to take an immense step into the unknown. It might lead to disaster. But it might open up unimagined new possibilities.

A Virginia planter and one of the most versatile men of his day, Thomas Jefferson is remembered as the chief author of the Declaration of Independence. This is a copy of a portrait by Rembrandt Peale, c. 1805.

One of the most controversial points in the original declaration was its condemnation of the slave trade. Though Jefferson owned slaves himself, he had deep misgivings about slavery as an institution. Yet the anti-slavery clause was stricken from the declaration's final draft. Though Americans talked of freedom, half a million men, women, and children remained in lifelong bondage.

At last the debating came to an end, and the final vote was taken. The Congress approved the document that separated America from Great Britain forever. The date was July 4, 1776.

The Declaration of Independence reflects Thomas Jefferson's passionate democratic principles. "We hold these truths to be self-evident," it states, "that all men are created equal; that they are endowed by their creator with certain unalienable rights; that among these are life, liberty, and the pursuit of happiness." More than two centuries have passed, but the words of the Declaration of Independence still shape the way we think of ourselves as individuals and as a nation.

## Defeated, But Not Destroyed

On July 9, Washington gathered his troops to hear the Declaration of Independence read aloud. Fervently he hoped that Jefferson's words would renew their courage for the struggle ahead. Early in April he had moved the Continental Army from Cambridge to New York, to prepare for the next confrontation of the war. But his

In June, 1776, Benjamin Franklin, Thomas Jefferson, John Adams,
Robert Livingston, and Roger Sherman met in Philadelphia to draft
the Declaration of Independence.

supplies of powder and ammunition were alarmingly low, and more men deserted every day. Now, British General William Howe was massing his forces on Staten Island, poised to attack.

To be ready for a British landing, Washington's men fortified the southern tip of Manhattan with walls and trenches. Then Washington decided to divide his army. While the main force remained on Manhattan, a smaller force of about 8,000 was ferried over the East River to Brooklyn Heights on Long Island.

General Howe, commander of the British troops in America, hoped to capture New York City, and then send his army north up the Hudson River to join British forces from Canada. By securing a corridor through New York, the British would separate the middle and southern colonies from New England. Then, rallying Loyalist support, Howe could drive the rebels from their last strongholds and win the war.

At dawn on August 22, Howe began the tedious process of moving horses, cannon, food, tents, and 15,000 men over the water to Gravesend Bay on Long Island. The Americans on Brooklyn Heights were seriously outnumbered. But they might have had a chance if it were not for the blundering of General John Sullivan. Known as the "Fighting Irishman," Sullivan was a feisty but incompetent officer. As he deployed the men under his command, he left a key road undefended. Meeting no opposition, the British marched in behind the rebel lines.

During most of the American Revolution, New York City was in the
hands of the British.

The Americans fought with fierce desperation, but from the start the British had the upper hand. By noon of August 27 the British flag flew proudly over Brooklyn Heights. "It was a fine sight to see with what alacrity [we] dispatched the rebels with bayonets after we had surrounded them so they could not resist," a British officer wrote a week later. "Multitudes were drowned and suffocated in morasses—a proper punishment for all rebels. . . . I expect the affair will be over this campaign, and we shall all . . . have the cream of American lands allotted us for our services."[7]

Reinforced by troops from Manhattan, Washington made a last attempt to recapture Brooklyn Heights. But by August 29, he realized that he must evacuate Long Island if he hoped to save what remained of his army. He called on two Massachusetts regiments, men experienced with small boats and treacherous seas. In the midst of a raging storm, the New Englanders ferried 9,500 men and most of their supplies back to Manhattan. When the sun finally broke through the clouds, Howe discovered that the rebels had slipped from his grasp. Washington may be held responsible for the disastrous defeat in the Battle of Long Island. But he also engineered the daring escape that spared his army so that they might fight again.

Late in September, British patrols challenged a young man named Nathan Hale on a quiet Manhattan road. Hale claimed to be a schoolteacher, but a careful search revealed a secret letter hidden in the sole of his

After a devastating defeat, Washington led his army to safety on August 28, 1776.

boot. The letter contained information about British troop movements on Long Island. Nathan Hale was hanged as a spy on September 22, 1776. According to accounts written a few years later, his last words were, "I only regret that I have but one life to lose for my country."

*I tell you with a heart not tenderly affected that this morning an express comes in with orders from the governor for my dearest beloved to march forthwith to New York with a part of his regiment, there to await the arrival of General Washington. What I have long feared is now come upon me. I endeavor to commit him to the care of a kind Providence, hoping he may be returned in safety.*

—Mary Fish Silliman, wife of a colonel of the Connecticut militia, in a letter to her parents, March 21, 1776.[1]

# 4 Beyond the Battlefield

 When Nathan Hale was hanged as a rebel spy, he became a celebrated hero of the revolution. But few remember Moses Dunbar of Wallingford, Connecticut, another young man whose passion for a cause was rewarded by the gallows. Like Hale, Dunbar was loyal to his country—but he felt that his country was England, not America. When war broke out, he tried to win recruits to fight with the British. He was captured by zealous neighbors and hanged as a traitor.

## Loyalists and Patriots

No one knows for certain how many Americans remained loyal to Great Britain. John Adams estimated that about one-third of the colonists were dedicated patriots, one-third were Loyalists, and the remaining third were committed to neither side. Over the course of the war, as many as 30,000 Americans fought with the British. Others sold food to the King's armies and reported on rebel troop movements.

Many families were torn apart by fierce differences over the war. Benjamin Franklin signed the Declaration of Independence; his son William, Royal Governor of New Jersey, was a staunch Loyalist. Father and son had once been very close, but their political disagreements led to a permanent break between them.

Loyalists (or Tories, as the patriots called them) often suffered brutal punishment. Their property was confiscated to help pay patriot war expenses. Many were driven from the communities where they had lived all their lives. Some were hanged, whipped, or tarred and feathered.

Ann Hulton, sister of a British official in Boston, saw a man tarred and feathered early in 1774.

> He was stripped stark naked on one of the severest cold nights this winter, his body covered all over with tar, then with feathers, his arm dislocated in tearing off his clothes. He was dragged in a cart with thousands attending, some beating him with clubs and knocking him out of the cart, then in again. They gave him several severe whippings at different parts of the town. This spectacle of horror and sport of cruelty was exhibited for about five hours. The unhappy

In New England, many men and women who sympathized with the British were tarred and feathered as punishment.

wretch they say behaved with the greatest intrepidity and fortitude all the while.[2]

Loyalists were most active in Georgia and the Carolinas, and in the middle colonies of New York, New Jersey, and Pennsylvania. In New Jersey's Hackensack Valley the tension between Loyalists and patriots (or Whigs, as the Loyalists called them) flared into outright warfare. Neighbors turned their muskets on one another and burned each other's houses and barns. No one and nothing was safe.

According to some historians, the American Revolution was actually the nation's first civil war. Like the War Between the States, it wrenched families apart and twisted old friends into bitter enemies. As passions mounted, the rules of decency crumbled. A spirit of distrust swept the colonies, turning ordinary people into accused and accusers.

Thousands of reasonable, sincere men and women wholeheartedly believed that the colonies should become independent. Thousands more, just as reasonable and sincere, felt that independence would lead to disaster. Risking their homes, their property, and even their lives, they pledged their loyalty to England.

## Hard Times at Home

Like hoards of locusts, the revolutionary armies devoured everything in their path as they moved from town to town. British and American soldiers alike stripped fields of their crops and emptied barns and storehouses. More than fifty years later, a farmer named Richard Durfee wrote the following account of life in Rhode Island in 1779, when the war was at its height:

> The beasts of the plow had been carried off by the enemy from the shore, or were removed into the back country out of their reach, or had been converted to food for the use of our own army; and if from some favorable circumstances the farmer could plant anything, he was . . . in constant jeopardy of losing [his crop] through the hostile attacks of the enemy on one side . . . and on the other side by the numerous wants and necessities of our own army . . . At that time some people were under the necessity of grinding flaxseed and cobs together to make bread . . . Our dwelling-houses were converted into barracks by the American army; our gardens, meadows, and tilled fields (such as we had) hardly furnished the necessary forage for the horses of the troops of our own army; and this state of things drove away all the arts, occupations, and comforts of peace.[3]

To make a bad situation truly desperate, inflation soared. The Continental Congress issued paper money that was almost worthless. People in the towns and cities, who could not grow their own food, could not afford the barest necessities sold in the market.

Hunger was a constant, looming threat. One woman wrote that she was "afraid to open my eyes on the day-light, lest I should hear my infant cry for bread and not have it in my power to relieve him. The first meal I have eaten for three days at one time was a morsel of dry bread and a lump of ice."[4]

At times the plundering of the armies came not from necessity, but from a breakdown of the rules that governed society. In September, 1777, a minister was asked to perform a child's funeral service. But when he reached the church, he found it occupied by the Pennsylvania Militia. He wrote:

> The floor was filled with straw and dirt, and on the altar they had their victuals, . . . I went in, but did not think it prudent to say anything to the crowd, as they began to mock, and some of the officers called out to [a man] playing the organ to play a Hessian march. I asked [the officer in command] if this was the promised protection to religious and civil freedom. He excused himself by saying that it was difficult to keep up strict discipline with the militia, who were composed of men of all nations. . . . I left a message for the parents of the dead child in such circumstances I could not attend the funeral or hold a discourse in the church for their consolation.[5]

While their husbands, fathers, and sons were fighting, women managed farms and businesses. Many found themselves cooking and washing for the soldiers quartered in their homes. Some took the opportunity to spy on enemy officers, secretly reporting any information they could gather about military plans.

Many women left home and followed their husbands to the army. They marched along with the troops, preparing meals, washing clothes, and nursing the sick and wounded. General Washington heartily disapproved, but he knew that desertions would increase if he sent the women away.

Though the revolution expanded the horizons of many women, the war exacted a cruel price. Hatred and killing undermined the most basic human compassion on both sides. One woman was aghast when she learned that Washington had refused Howe a three-day cease-fire to care for the wounded and bury the dead. "What a woeful tendency war has, to harden the human heart against the tender feelings of humanity. Well may it be called a horrid art, thus to change the nature of man."[6]

## The Sick and the Wounded

During the Revolutionary War, the hospital was far more dangerous than the battlefield. Disease killed six of every seven men who died in the conflict. Smallpox, dysentery, typhoid, and typhus flourished in filthy, crowded army barracks.

Doctors in the eighteenth century believed that the human body was composed of four substances, or humors—earth, air, water, and fire. When these humors were out of balance, illness resulted. The treatment to restore balance was often worse than the disease itself.

One of the most popular medical practices during the war years was bleeding. The doctor opened a patient's vein, or applied blood-sucking leeches to the sick person's body. He hoped to rid the patient of dangerous impurities in this way. In another treatment, harsh substances were applied to the skin to cause blisters. It was thought that these blisters would somehow counteract irritants within the person's body, thus bringing about a cure. The only known painkillers were alcohol and laudanum, the latter being derived from the opium poppy.

Although they had no idea that microorganisms caused disease, doctors did have a method of inoculating against smallpox. Fluid was taken from the pustule of a smallpox patient and scraped into the skin of a healthy person. After this treatment, the healthy person usually developed a mild case of the disease and was then immune to further attacks. Since some people died from the inoculation itself, the procedure was very controversial. However, General Washington encouraged inoculation in an effort to control the epidemics that ravaged the Continental Army.

In 1775 the Continental Congress established an army medical corps known as the Hospital. From the outset, the Hospital was plagued with problems. Its first director general turned out to be a British spy, and another was accused of stealing army medical supplies. There were never enough blankets, food, or medicines, and never enough doctors and nurses to care for the sick and wounded men who crowded hospital tents.

The most famous physician of the American Revolution was Dr. Benjamin Rush of Philadelphia. Rush was an ardent patriot and a signer of the Declaration of Independence. He was impressed by the cleanliness and efficiency of British army hospitals, and worked valiantly to improve conditions in American medical facilities. He encouraged the troops to bathe regularly and to eat a diet of fresh vegetables. He also took an unpopular stand against tobacco and rum. In 1778 Rush resigned after a bitter quarrel with his superior. More than a century would pass before his ideas gained wide acceptance by the medical profession.

## Prisoners of War

In battles and skirmishes throughout the war, both sides took prisoners. But these captured men had to be fed, sheltered, and prevented from escaping or rioting. Neither the Americans nor the British were in any position to care for the thousands of men they held in custody. They had few resources to spare—all their men and provisions were needed for the fighting.

Both the British and the Americans claimed that they treated prisoners honorably, according to the accepted codes of warfare. But both sides committed horrible atrocities.

The most notorious British war prisons were the "hulks," great ships anchored in the Hudson River. Thousands of Americans languished in the dark, airless holds deep below the water line of the prison ships. There was seldom enough food or fresh water to go around, and epidemics of smallpox and other diseases raged. Historians estimate that 7,000 patriots died aboard the hulks before the war was over.

William Slade, a young volunteer from Connecticut, managed to keep a diary during his months aboard the prison ship *Grosvenor*. His brief entries give a chilling glimpse into prison life.

Last night was spent in dying groans and cries. I now grow poorly. Terrible storm as ever I saw. High wind. At noon meat and peas. Very cold and stormy. . . . Three men of our battalion died last night. The most melancholiest night I ever saw. Smallpox increases fast. This day I was blooded. Stomach all gone.[7]

Constantly on the move, the Americans had no time to establish large, permanent prisons. They housed prisoners in churches, warehouses, barracks, and even abandoned mines. The most infamous American prison was the Simmsbury Copper Mine at East Granby, Connecticut. The prisoners descended by a series of ladders into dark caverns 30 yards below the earth's surface. Most of the prisoners confined at East Granby were Loyalists. Among them was William Franklin, Benjamin Franklin's son.

Throughout the war, diplomats tried to arrange prisoner exchanges, or to negotiate for some prisoners to be freed on the promise that they would not fight again. But neither side trusted the other. In most cases, negotiations broke down. No one knows for certain how many died while they waited for the fighting to be over.

## Across the Atlantic

While the revolution was fought with muskets and cannon in America, in England's Parliament the weapons were words. Some of the nation's most eloquent speakers championed the American point of view. But the King and Parliament's conservative members stood firm. The colonies were too valuable to throw away.

Thousands of American prisoners of war were confined on British ships anchored in New York Harbor.

In the airless hold of a British prison ship, men were constantly threatened by hunger and disease.

They must be taught a lesson. They must remain part of the British Empire.

Many ordinary people believed the war was necessary to rescue the good Americans (the Loyalists) from the bad ones (the patriots). But the war also caused severe hardships in England. Merchants grumbled that it interrupted their profitable trade with the colonies. Homemakers complained about soaring prices in the market. Nearly everyone was indignant over the rise in taxes. But nothing angered the people so much as the impressment of sailors for the British navy.

For centuries, the British navy had used "press gangs" to round up new recruits. These gangs of ruffians kidnapped unfortunate young men on the streets and in the taverns and carried them off to waiting ships. Years might pass before they saw their families again—if they managed to return at all. The American Revolution found the British fighting French and Spanish warships and American privateers that attacked English vessels with the approval of the Continental Congress. Desperate for recruits, the British navy resorted to impressment once again. The navy even seized sailors from British merchant ships. As the conflict wore on, proud trading vessels floated at anchor, empty and abandoned.

Many people in Britain objected to the war on philosophical grounds. As one antiwar pamphlet argued:

> Have [the Americans] crossed the ocean and invaded us? Have they attempted to take from us the fruits of our labor, and to overturn that form of government which we hold so sacred? . . . On

Despite warnings from many of the ablest members of Parliament, King George III refused to change his repressive attitude toward the American colonies. According to legend, he was insane.

the contrary, this is what we have done to them. . . . Would we but let them alone . . . they would thank and bless us; and yet it is we who imagine ourselves ill-used.

King George III was unable to understand how the colonists felt, or to recognize the widespread unpopularity of the war among his own people at home. He was determined to "save the empire," to rescue British honor in the eyes of the world. He could imagine no other course of action but to pour more and more lives and money into the war in America.

How happy the soldier who lives on his pay
And spends half-a-crown out of sixpence a day;
Yet fears neither justices, warrants nor bums,
But pays all his debts with the roll of his drums.
With row de dow, row de dow, row de dow dow,
And pays all his debts with the roll of his drums.

—Popular British marching song

# 5 Shifting the Balance

 With their poor food, crowded living quarters, and nonexistent sanitation, military camps were a breeding-ground for disease. Defeated soldiers seemed especially vulnerable, and Washington's army was no exception. After the defeat on Long Island, epidemics raged among the demoralized troops. Men fell to dysentery and smallpox. The wounded burned with fever from vicious infections. But the army had to keep moving, for the British were in close pursuit.

## A Surprise for Christmas

In September of 1776, Washington's men withdrew to the northern end of Manhattan and beat the British in a series of skirmishes at Harlem Heights. In October,

George Washington and General William Howe clashed again, at White Plains, New York. Washington was forced to retreat once more.

In November, General Howe captured Fort Washington on the east side of the Hudson. Within days another British general, Lord Charles Cornwallis, took Fort Lee in New Jersey. The Americans lost artillery pieces and other vital supplies, and some 2,000 men were captured. With his last 3,000 troops, Washington set out across New Jersey in full retreat. General Cornwallis wrote gleefully that he would soon bag the rebel leader like a fox. But the Americans were at their best with quick maneuvers and lightning raids. "As we go forward into the country the rebels fly before us, and when we come back they always follow us," one British officer wrote in dismay. "Tis almost impossible to catch them."

At last, on December 7, Washington crossed the Delaware into Pennsylvania. His men took or destroyed every boat they could find along the river. By the time Howe reached the Delaware, not even a canoe was to be found to ferry his army to the other side. Washington had escaped once again.

It was a long-standing tradition of European warfare that fighting stopped during the winter. In keeping with this ancient custom, Howe turned away from the Delaware and set off for the comfort of winter quarters in New York. He left New Jersey under General James Grant and his Hessian soldiers. The Hessians were German troops who sold their services to the British army. Most Americans, even those loyal to the Crown,

Lord Charles Cornwallis pursued George Washington's Continental Army across New Jersey.

resented these "foreigners" who came to fight against the colonists.

The Continental Army desperately needed a victory, and Washington was determined to provide one. On Christmas night he ordered 2,400 men to re-cross the Delaware for a surprise attack on the Hessian garrison at Trenton. Loaded with men and supplies, boats fought through high winds and floating ice chunks to the New Jersey side. Once they clambered ashore, the men faced a nine-mile march in the biting cold. But at last, early on the morning of December 26, they marched into Trenton.

Most of the Hessians had spent the previous day in holiday merrymaking. Now they tumbled out of bed to the roar of guns in the streets. They barely had time to load their muskets before the Americans were upon them. Henry Knox, the engineer who had brought the cannon from Ticonderoga, described the scene in a letter to his wife:

> The hurry, fright, and confusion of the enemy was not unlike that which will be when the last trumpet shall sound. . . . [Our cannons and howitzers] in the twinkling of an eye cleared the streets. . . . Finally they were driven through the town into an open plain beyond. . . . The poor fellows saw themselves completely surrounded. . . . They were obliged to surrender on the spot with all their artillery, six brass pieces, army colors, etc. . . . Great advantages may be gained from it if we take the proper steps.[1]

On Christmas night, 1776, Washington led his troops across the icy Delaware River and launched a surprise attack on the Hessian soldiers at Trenton, New Jersey.

With only five casualties on their side (including two men who froze to death on the march), the Americans crossed back to Pennsylvania. Ten days later, Washington led his men to a brilliant victory over the British at Princeton, New Jersey.

Trenton and Princeton were not important military prizes. But the patriots turned these small victories to great advantage, as Henry Knox foretold. The triumphs at Trenton and Princeton provided the morale boost the weary Continental soldiers needed to keep fighting.

## Turning the Tide

"We have a pretty amusement by the name of foraging, or fighting for our daily bread," a British officer wrote in February, 1777. Quartered in taverns and houses in New York, Howe's army faced a long, hungry winter. Soldiers stole cows and chickens from farmers' barns, and raided families' winter stores of potatoes, corn, and other vegetables. As the months passed, even some of the staunchest New York Loyalists turned against the British. Washington's troops, wintering in Morristown, New Jersey, were almost as unpopular. Though Washington ordered that farmers must be paid for food, plenty of foraging went on. Worse still, the army brought smallpox, and Washington turned private homes into infirmaries.

Warm weather found both armies on the move again. Now the British pushed toward Philadelphia, the rebel capital. In September, Howe's forces swept aside American resistance at Brandywine Creek in Pennsylvania.

Two weeks later, the British poured into General Anthony Wayne's camp at Paoli, Pennsylvania, in the dead of night. Not a shot was fired. Slashing and jabbing with their razor-sharp bayonets, the British killed some 300 Continental soldiers, many still wrapped in their blankets. The assault is remembered today as the Paoli Massacre.

Howe's troops soon overran Philadelphia. The Continental Congress escaped to nearby York, Pennsylvania. Washington tried to recapture Philadelphia, but he was defeated at the village of Germantown.

On a visit to England months before, General John Burgoyne bet a friend that he would return from America victorious within a year. Burgoyne was an ambitious man, but he was plagued by gambling debts. Hoping to win both money and fame, he devised a plan that he was

In 1777, the British captured Philadelpia, seat of the Continental Congress.

sure could not fail. He would capture the town of Albany and establish a chain of forts along the Hudson to New York City. There he would join forces with Howe. Rallying the Loyalists, they would win the southern colonies and end the war at last.

Just as he expected, Burgoyne easily recaptured Crown Point and Ticonderoga. In high spirits the expedition headed south. Again and again Burgoyne told his men, "This army must never retreat."

Burgoyne's 6,000 fighting men included British and German regular soldiers, American Loyalists, and about 80 Oneida Indians. The army did not travel light. Heavy supply wagons ground slowly along twisting muddy roads. Horse-drawn cannons tangled in the underbrush. Some of the officers had brought their wives along, and even their children.

On Bemis Heights, a bluff overlooking the Hudson, General Horatio Gates waited with the northern branch of the Continental Army. A cautious man by nature, Gates planned to hold back until Burgoyne came within striking distance. But among his supporting generals was the irrepressible Benedict Arnold. Arnold finally persuaded Gates to attack when Burgoyne reached the land of a nearby farmer named Freeman.

For hours under a blazing September sun, Col. Daniel Morgan's Virginia riflemen fought the British for a tiny clearing on Freeman's Farm. Against Gates' orders, Benedict Arnold rushed into the battle, fighting with a madman's fury. Burgoyne held the clearing, but his losses were disastrous.

On October 7, Burgoyne sent a reconnaissance party of 1,500 men to survey the area around Bemis Heights. While some of the soldiers followed orders, others took the opportunity to harvest a field of wheat. It had been a long time since they had tasted fresh bread. Suddenly the Americans struck. Once again Arnold defied Gates' orders and flung himself into the action. The Americans cheered as he rode up and down, shouting orders, thrusting with his sword, seeming to be everywhere at once.

At last, against his deepest principles, Burgoyne withdrew from Bemis Heights to Saratoga. The Americans kept up a relentless pursuit. In her diary Baroness von Riedhesel, wife of the leading German commander, described the last agonizing days of the campaign. She and her children hid in the cellar of a farmhouse, along with dozens of wounded men. "Eleven cannonballs went through the house, and we could plainly hear them rolling over our heads. One poor soldier whose leg they were about to amputate . . . had the other leg taken off by a cannonball in the very middle of the operation."[2]

At Saratoga, Burgoyne's forces found themselves surrounded by 17,000 American soldiers. Finally, on October 17, Gates and Burgoyne signed a truce, and the British lay down their arms. After all the bloodshed, the generals treated each other with the utmost courtesy. "The fortunes of war, general, have made me your prisoner," Burgoyne told Gates, raising his hat. Gates replied, "I shall always be ready to bear testimony that it has not been through any fault of your excellency." The generals and their top officers then sat down together

American forces under General Horatio Gates defeated British General John Burgoyne at Saratoga in October, 1778. The battle is sometimes called the turning-point of the war.

over roast beef and glasses of wine. Giddy with exhaustion, they were soon joking and laughing as though they were old friends. They seemed to forget the men who had lost their lives, and the hundreds who still groaned in pain. One British artillery major was struck by the strange behavior of the people around him when he remarked that it certainly was "an odd old world."

# Help from Afar

On an autumn day in 1776, a bespectacled American gentleman in a coonskin cap stepped down from a carriage in Paris. People crowded the street, eager to catch a glimpse of the great American philosopher and inventor, Benjamin Franklin. Franklin was seventy years old and in failing health when the Continental Congress sent him to France to enlist French support for the revolution. From the first, he was enormously popular there. His picture appeared on shaving mugs, snuffboxes, and the handles of pocketknives. Paris hostesses vied with one another for his time and attention. To the French people, Franklin represented an honest, homespun simplicity, and a faith in the democratic principles that they themselves had begun to embrace. (France would overthrow its own king and set up a republic in 1789 during the French Revolution.)

For generations, France and England had glared at one another across the English Channel. Since 1700, they had gone to war four times. With its sprawling empire and mighty navy, Britain constantly seemed to

Scientist and inventor, writer and philosopher, businessman and diplomat, Benjamin Franklin was one of the greatest geniuses America has ever produced.

thwart French ambitions. Yet France was reluctant to face the expense of another war it was bound to lose.

Without official government approval, many French citizens aided the American war effort. The flamboyant playwright Caron de Beaumarchais organized business-men to send shipments of guns and ammunition. In 1777 a young French nobleman, the Marquis de La-fayette, offered his enthusiastic service to the Continental Army. When he was only nineteen, he was appointed a major general. His bravery and dedication won him Washington's respect and earned him the love of the pa-triots.

Meanwhile, the diplomats smiled and bowed, and France stayed out of the war. The French would not commit themselves to the conflict unless they believed the colonies could win.

The breakthrough finally came in November, 1777, when Paris learned of Burgoyne's defeat at Saratoga. The whole northern branch of the British army had been captured—seven generals, 300 officers, and more than 5,000 men. At last the French had the hard evidence they demanded. The American rebels just might have a chance after all.

In a quiet ceremony on February 6, 1778, France and America signed a military alliance. Soon the French navy was fighting the British on the high seas, and ship-loads of French soldiers and supplies landed at American ports. A year later, Spain also entered the war against Great Britain. The Netherlands, too, offered its support to the American cause. The conflict that had first erupted over stamps and tea now swept with deadly fervor across the western world.

## Coming Through the Hard Times

Philadelphia, once the American capital, lay in the grip of the British. To keep a close watch on the enemy, General Washington set up winter quarters at the village of Valley Forge, only 18 miles away. Above the encampment was a wooded hill called Mount Joy. After a few weeks at Valley Forge, the soldiers joked that it should have been called Mount Misery.

By mid-December, 1777, the woods around Valley Forge rang with the sound of axes as the men chopped down trees and split logs with which to build huts for the winter. As there were no nails to be had, the logs were fitted together with notches. Some of the huts had no flooring but the ground, and even straw for bedding was lacking.

For months the soldiers had worn the same clothes every day, and by now what was left of them hung in tatters. Many of the men no longer had shirts or trousers and had to wrap themselves in blankets. When their boots fell to pieces, they struggled barefoot through the snow. On watch, they stood in their hats. Countless soldiers lost their feet to frostbite.

The farms around Valley Forge produced plenty of food, but most of it found its way to Philadelphia. The British could pay for food with hard cash, while Washington had only the worthless paper money issued

General George Washington and his army endured severe hunger and cold at Valley Forge, Pennsylvania, through the winter of 1777-78.

by the Continental Congress. Washington's men lived on water and firecake—a heavy, tasteless bread baked on stones in the fireplace. Once, for a special treat, each man received four ounces of rice and a tablespoon of vinegar.

In February 1778, a new volunteer arrived in camp. He was Baron Friedrich Wilhelm von Steuben, who said he had been a general in the Prussian army. With a letter of recommendation from Benjamin Franklin, he had come to help train Washington's army.

Every morning von Steuben rose at three o'clock to begin the day's work. The Americans did not know the most basic maneuvers. He even had to show them the correct way to stand at attention. He taught the men to march in formation and to handle their weapons effectively. Because von Steuben spoke little English, another officer interpreted his orders. At times, driven by frustration, the baron would turn to his interpreter and tell him to curse at the men in English for him.

The men liked and respected von Steuben, and gradually his drilling paid off. The capture of two British supply ships yielded enough woolen uniforms to clothe most of the troops. By May, one observer wrote admiringly of "the air of our soldiers, the cleanliness of their dress, the brilliancy and good order of their arms, and the remarkable animation with which they performed the necessary salute as the general passed along. Indeed, during the whole review, the utmost military decorum was preserved."[3]

Eventually, Washington learned that von Steuben

Baron Friedrich von Steuben was an invaluable asset to General Washington. He shaped a ragged horde of Continental soldiers into a formidable army.

had never been a general in Prussia, only a captain. Washington did not care. He appointed von Steuben major general, and treated him with all the regard due a trusted friend and ally.

In June 1778, messengers galloped into camp with astonishing news. The British were abandoning Philadelphia! At first no one believed them. But loaded supply wagons were rumbling out of the city. General Howe had resigned and returned to England, leaving General Henry Clinton in command of the British forces. Clinton did not like Philadelphia. He feared that a rebel blockade could cut off supplies. Clinton determined to combine the forces in Philadelphia with those already established in New York.

Once the British had pursued Washington across New Jersey. Now Washington set off in pursuit of the British. He had 11,000 men, equal to the enemy force. He hoped to deliver a crushing blow before the British reached their New York stronghold.

Slowly, clumsily, the two great armies lumbered over the New Jersey countryside. As usual, the British were loaded down more heavily than the Americans. A trail of supply wagons 12 miles long straggled behind the main body of soldiers. As the days passed, Washington drew closer and closer. At last, when the British reached the village of Monmouth, the two armies lay within striking range.

In command of his advance guard Washington placed General Charles Lee of Virginia. Lee, who had spent fifteen months as a British prisoner, was not enthusiastic about this campaign. But he set out with 5,000 men, under orders to attack Clinton's rear guard. Washington would catch up to support him with the rest of the army.

From the beginning, Lee seemed confused and reluctant. "Our men were formed piecemeal in front of the enemy, and there seemed to be no general plan or disposition," wrote an officer from South Carolina. "One order succeeded another with a rapidity and indecision calculated to ruin us."[4] As the British turned to resist their attackers, Lee pulled back in a ragged retreat.

When Washington realized what had happened, he "swore till the leaves shook on the trees," in the words of one witness. He galloped forward, shouting orders, and swung the Americans back into formation. Lee took charge of the advance lines once more, and the Battle of Monmouth raged on.

A merciless June sun beat down, and the temperature soared to 100 degrees. Men and horses collapsed from the heat while muskets and cannon roared around them. In the thick of the fighting, a young woman hurried up and down the American lines, bringing water to the exhausted soldiers. Her name was Mary Hays, the wife of Pvt. John Hays, but the men called her Molly Pitcher. When her husband was killed, she took his place at the cannon. Once a British ball flew between her knees and tore away part of her petticoat, but she fought on without flinching.

Mary Hays was known as Molly Pitcher because she carried water to thirsty Continental soldiers during the Battle of Monmouth. When her husband was killed, she took his place at the cannon.

When night fell on June 28, the shelling slowly subsided. The British and the Americans had each suffered about 350 casualties. Under cover of darkness, the British quietly slipped away. Washington did not chase them any further. He had shown them what his men could do. For now, that was enough.

I must study politics and war that my sons may
have liberty to study mathematics and philosophy.
My sons ought to study mathematics and
philosophy . . . in order to give their children a
right to study painting, poetry, music, architecture,
statuary, tapestry, and porcelain.

—John Adams, in a letter to his wife, Abigail Adams,
May 12, 1780

# 6

# The Final Act

 To the west of the warring colonies—from
New York to Georgia—stretched vast un-
tamed forests and plains with only a scattering of white
settlements. During the war the powerful Iroquois Indians and their allies sided with the British, who had
promised to stop American expansion.

## Battles on the Frontier

In the summer of 1778, British regulars, Loyalists, and
Indians attacked the isolated farms and villages in Pennsylvania's Wyoming Valley. Hundreds of men, women,
and children were killed—many of them tortured and
scalped. According to one newspaper account, "They
[then] proceeded to the destruction of every building
and improvement (except what belonged to some

Tories) that came within their reach throughout all these flourishing settlements, which they have rendered a scene of desolation and horror almost beyond description."[1]

A few months later, the British and Indians massacred settlers at Cherry Valley, New York. Leading the raiding party was a Mohawk chief known by the Christian name Joseph Brant. Brant had been educated at a school for Indian children in Connecticut and later received formal military training in England. He was not only a skillful leader on the battlefield, but a zealous missionary for the Episcopal Church.

Much of the land along the Ohio River was disputed by Virginia and Great Britain. George Rogers Clark, a young surveyor and Indian fighter, was determined to drive the British from this region, commonly known as the Northwest Territory. In July 1778, with a band of only 200 men, Clark seized three key forts—Kaskaskia and Cahokia in present-day Illinois, and Vincennes in present-day Indiana. But Vincennes soon fell again to the British under William Henry Hamilton, the territory's British governor.

To the Americans on the frontier, Hamilton was the "Hair-Buyer" who paid the Indians for settlers' scalps. Clark resolved to recapture Fort Vincennes, though his forces were hopelessly outnumbered. "I know the case is desperate," he wrote to Patrick Henry, now governor of Virginia, "but sir, we must either quit the country, or attack Mr. Hamilton. . . . Great things have been affected by a few men well conducted. Perhaps we may be fortunate."[2]

In February, 1779, George Rogers Clark braved the perils of the
frontier to recapture the fort at Vincennes from the British.

After slogging across the winter prairie for more than two weeks, Clark took Vincennes completely by surprise on February 23, 1779. Soon after the fighting began, a group of unsuspecting Indians approached the fort. At once Clark and his men made them prisoners. "I had now a fair opportunity of making an impression on the Indians, . . . that of convincing them that Governor Hamilton could not give them that protection that he had made them to believe he could," Clark wrote months later. "In some measure to incense the Indians against him for not exerting himself to save their friends, I ordered the prisoners to be tomahawked in the face of the garrison."[3] As Clark hoped, Hamilton's Indian allies turned against him. Clark soon possessed Vincennes once more.

When Clark sat down to discuss the terms of peace, his face and hands were still spattered with enemy blood. Even Hair-Buyer Hamilton was appalled by Clark's barbarous treatment of his captives. After his final surrender he lamented his "mortification, disappointment and indignation" at having to yield to an unprincipled crew of bandits.

## War on the High Seas

It has often been said that war is the mother of invention. The American Revolution "invented" the world's first submarine. Developed by David Bushnell, a Connecticut engineer, it somewhat resembled an enormous turtle. Its hull was made from great slabs of oak, encircled by heavy iron bands, and caulked with tar. A lone man served as captain and crew, pumping water out to raise the vessel or in to lower it. He steered by means of a crank, which in turn maneuvered a set of paddles.

In 1776, the submarine set out to blow up a British ship in New York Harbor. The captain managed to deposit an underwater bomb—a wooden shell packed with powder—set to explode in half an hour. But the current carried the bomb away from its target. It blew up harmlessly in the East River with a spectacular roar and a shower of splinters.

To the British, the American navy seemed even less a threat than Bushnell's turtle. Britain had ruled the seas for more than two centuries. America's navy was born in 1775, and it began with only five armed vessels. As the war progressed, however, the Continental navy grew in strength. American frigates fought fierce battles at sea, and on a few occasions even attacked British ports.

American privateers proved to be an even greater menace. These were privately owned vessels that were licensed by Congress to capture enemy ships. The British called privateering a legalized form of piracy. "[The] wretches with which their privateers are manned have no principles whatever," wrote one British admiral. "They live by piracy and the plunder of their fellow subjects. When they have been released . . . to return to their families and live by honest industry, they . . . instantly return to renew their acts of piracy."[4]

Some 200 British vessels were sunk or captured by the Continental navy, and privateers claimed at least 600 more. Of all the sea battles of the war, one lives on as legend—the deadly combat between the British warship *Serapis* and *Bonhomme Richard* commanded by Captain John Paul Jones.

The *Bonhomme Richard* clashed with the *Serapis* on September 23, 1779, off the coast of England. The *Serapis* was escorting 40 British merchantmen, who quickly sailed for cover when the fighting began. Jones' ship was not as well armed as the *Serapis,* and his men had less experience. But Jones was a fearless fighter who did not believe in defeat.

Early in the battle, a shell from the *Serapis* detonated powder kegs on the *Richard's* deck and killed many of Jones' best men. But Jones locked the two ships together with giant grappling hooks. They fought side to side in a haze of smoke and flame. Riflemen on the *Richard* picked off every British sailor in sight, until the survivors fled below decks. But the *Richard* was taking on water and seemed about to sink. Captain Pearson of the *Serapis* called to Jones and asked if he was ready to surrender. Over the roar of gunfire Jones shouted back, "I have not yet begun to fight!"

At last the *Serapis'* mainmast toppled, and Pearson hauled down the ensign in surrender. Not only had Jones captured the *Serapis,* he had struck a symbolic blow against the British navy, the heart of England's power.

## The War Moves South

At his headquarters in New York City, General Henry Clinton studied his maps. The rebels were strong from

In a dramatic and bloody battle on September 23, 1779, Captain John Paul Jones captured the British warship *Serapis*.

New England through the middle colonies, as far south as Virginia. But plenty of Loyalists were still active in Georgia and the Carolinas. If the British marched south, surely they could rally support along the way and turn the tide of the war.

In 1776, Clinton had tried unsuccessfully to take Charleston, South Carolina, the largest city in the south. Now, in November 1778, Clinton sent Col. Archibald Campbell south with 3,500 Loyalists and British regulars. With one swift blow they captured the city of Savannah, and within a month all Georgia was in British hands. Clinton's plan seemed to be working.

Late in December 1779, Clinton set sail from New York to South Carolina with General Charles Cornwallis and a fleet of 90 transports and 14 warships. For four weeks, they were pummeled by fierce Atlantic storms. Masts cracked, sails flapped in shreds, and several ships went to the bottom. "Always the same weather," one soldier wrote in his diary. "Storm, rain, hail, snow, and the waves breaking over the cabin."

After the troops finally landed, they spent another ten days trudging through marshes before they reached their destination. A city of handsome brick mansions and more modest wooden houses, Charleston, South Carolina, was home to some 12,000 whites and almost as many slaves. Although many of the inhabitants were loyal to England, the rebels had already built walls and dug trenches. The British, too, began to dig and build, protecting their position outside the city.

The siege got underway in April. At the beginning, British and American soldiers faced each other from rows of trenches 800 yards apart. By day the British pounded the city with artillery fire. By night they dug fresh trenches, creeping ever closer to the enemy lines. The soil was loose, wet, and sandy. Sometimes the men crouched in water, and nearly always they were tormented by stinging sand fleas.

The British became easier targets the nearer they came. The Americans made bombs by packing canisters with broken bits of shovels, axes, and guns. When the canisters exploded, these fragments flew out in all directions, inflicting ghastly wounds. The British hurled back deadly mortar shells and bombs filled with bullets. Fires raged through the town. At last, on May 12, 1780, Charleston surrendered to the British.

In the months that followed, North and South Carolina seethed with fighting. In the mountainous "back country," Whigs murdered Tories and Tories murdered Whigs. No one was safe. No property was spared.

After the victory at Charleston, General Clinton returned to New York. The British forces in the south were now under the command of General Cornwallis. Cornwallis' task was not an easy one. Tough rebel bands under Thomas "Gamecock" Sumter and Francis Marion (known as the Swamp Fox) harassed the British throughout the woods and marshes. Many supposed Loyalists left the British camp to join these feisty partisan leaders.

In August 1780, General Horatio Gates set out

across hostile country to meet the British at Camden, South Carolina. Stores of food ran low on the long march, and many of the men became sick from eating unripe corn and green peaches. Ill and exhausted, they broke ranks and scattered at General Cornwallis' first charge. "I confess that I was amongst the first that fled," one militiaman wrote later. "The cause of that I cannot tell, except that everyone I saw was about to do the same. It was instantaneous. There was no effort to rally, no encouragement to fight."[5]

Still, the rebel attacks on British outposts and scouting parties continued. With a company of more than 1,000 Loyalists, a handsome Scottish major named Patrick Ferguson determined to put an end to the trouble. In October he met the rebels at Kings Mountain on a long ridge between North and South Carolina.

In typically British style, the Loyalists fired in volleys and made massed charges with drawn bayonets. But Kings Mountain was the kind of setting where the "overmountain men" of the back country did their best fighting. Crouching behind trees and boulders, they picked off the Loyalists one by one. They darted forward, then slipped back out of sight. And all the time they scrambled higher and higher.

Fearlessly, Ferguson rushed into the noise and smoke on his magnificent white horse. A sudden barrage of bullets riddled his body, and he tumbled to the ground. The Loyalists surrendered, their gallant leader dead.

Inflamed by the madness of battle, the rebels shot wounded men who begged for mercy, and chased down

In May, 1780, British forces drove the Americans into a frenzied retreat at the Battle of Camden, South Carolina.

those who tried to crawl to safety. Sixteen-year-old James Collins recalled:

> The dead lay in heaps on all sides, while the groans of the wounded were heard in every direction. I could not help turning away from the scene before me with horror; and though exulting in victory could not refrain from shedding tears. . . . We proceeded to bury the dead, but it was badly done. They were thrown into convenient piles and covered with old logs, the bark of old trees, and rocks. . . . The wolves became so plenty that it was dangerous for anyone to be out at night for several miles round.[6]

## The World Turned Upside Down

Brilliant but chronically dissatisfied, Benedict Arnold quarreled endlessly with his fellow officers. He never felt that General Washington gave him proper recognition in the Continental Army. Over the summer of 1780 he spent more and more time with Loyalist friends in New York. In September he made a secret agreement with the British. For £20,000, English money, and a commission as major general in the British Army, Arnold promised to hand over the American fort at West Point to the enemy. His plans were discovered at the last minute, and Arnold barely escaped with his life. Three weeks before the Battle of King's Mountain, Washington received the shocking news—Benedict Arnold had turned traitor!

Arnold's treason was a severe blow to the Continental Army. But Washington, at his head quarters in New Jersey, had even graver concerns. Supplies were running

Though he was one of the most brilliant generals of the Continental Army, Benedict Arnold is chiefly remembered for turning traitor.

low again, and morale was sinking. But, a French fleet under Admiral de Grasse was sailing to America's aid. Here, perhaps was the opportunity to end the war with one decisive blow.

Meanwhile, General Nathanael Greene was fighting a hit-and-run war with Cornwallis across the Carolinas. At last Cornwallis reached Virginia and fortified the village of Yorktown, just up the York River from Chesapeake Bay. General Clinton promised to send reinforcements to Cornwallis by sea.

When he learned of Cornwallis' position, Washington decided to launch an attack. To mislead Clinton, he pretended he was preparing for a campaign in New York. He repaired roads and bridges and even built a giant oven to bake bread for the troops. Then, with a combined army of French and American troops, he headed for Virginia. He was joined by French Admiral de Grasse, who stationed 24 ships in Chesapeake Bay.

Cornwallis lacked men and supplies to withstand a long siege. As French and American soldiers encircled the town and began building fortifications, he waited for help from Clinton. But Clinton encountered one delay after another. Unaware of Cornwallis' real distress, he sent messages urging him to be patient. Yet day by day the enemy ramparts drew closer, like a tightening noose. A haze of smoke hung in the air, and the terrible noise of cannon was unrelenting.

In Yorktown, the human suffering grew unbearable as the siege dragged on. The British slaughtered horses to feed the hungry troops. Dead and wounded men lay heaped in the streets. The fate of the town's slaves was especially cruel. Sarah Osborn, an American woman who followed her husband throughout the war, remembered, "[I] saw a number of dead Negroes lying round [the British] encampment, whom [I] understood the British had driven out of the town and left to starve, or had first starved and then thrown out."[7]

At last Cornwallis realized reinforcements would not arrive. His only hope lay in retreat. But when he began to ferry his men across the York River to safety, a violent storm blew up. Even retreat had become impossible.

On the morning of October 17, a lone drummer boy appeared on the main British parapet. Beside him an officer held up a white handkerchief. Suddenly, the din of gunfire ceased. Sarah Osborn saw the American officers toss their hats in the air. "[I] asked them, 'What is the matter now?' One of them replied, 'Are not you soldier enough to know what it means? . . . The British have surrendered.'"[8]

Two days later the formal ceremony of surrender took place. Cornwallis' army filed slowly past General Washington, and one by one the soldiers dropped their muskets. Cornwallis did not appear at the ceremony. In his tent he wrote a letter to Clinton: "Under these circumstances I thought it would have been wanton and inhuman to the last degree to sacrifice the lives of this small body of gallant soldiers."[9]

The British band played fifes and drums wrapped in

On October 17, 1781, British Commander Lord Charles Cornwallis surrendered at Yorktown, Virginia. The Battle of Yorktown was the last major confrontation of the war.

black crepe. Strangely, for this somber occasion they chose a jaunty popular song called "The World Turned Upside Down." The world had indeed turned upside down in the course of the long war. Somehow a collection of colonies on the edge of the wilderness had defeated the most powerful nation on earth.

*There never was a good war or a bad peace.*
—Benjamin Franklin, 1773.

# 7 Shaping the Peace

Even after Lord Charles Cornwallis surrendered at Yorktown, British and American soldiers continued to clash in a series of bloody skirmishes. For two more years fighting flared in Pennsylvania and New Jersey, in Georgia and along the frontier. Although King George III still believed the colonies could be persuaded to surrender, Parliament and the British people were weary of the war. It was time to relinquish the American colonies and concentrate on more pressing matters at home.

Meanwhile in Paris, Benjamin Franklin, John Adams, and John Jay hammered out the terms of a peace treaty. American territory would extend as far west as the Mississippi River, and there would be no further harassment by the British. Franklin hoped to annex Canada, but in that matter the British would not yield. Above all, the American peace commission demanded that Great Britain recognize the former colonies as a new, independent nation—the United States of America.

At the same time, Britain made peace with its other enemies, France and Spain. The final treaty—The Treaty of Paris—was signed on September 3, 1783.

From New Hampshire to Georgia, men and women came home from a life of marches and army camps. Over the years that followed, they rebuilt ravaged farms and put behind them memories of hardship and suffering.

After the war, thousands of Loyalists left America for England. The British government helped them resettle, but most were homesick and discontented. They found British society too formal, its class structure too rigid. In the end, they discovered they were Americans at heart.

As they had hoped, some of the African Americans who fought in the war received their freedom. But many others were reclaimed by their masters. After years of service to the cause of freedom and independence they became slaves once more.

The struggle for American independence inspired a series of revolutions that shook the world for the next hundred years. In 1789, the people of France overthrew the aristocracy to found a republic. Slaves in Haiti revolted in 1804 and established an independent nation. Through a series of rebellions in the 1800's, Spain lost

Painted by Archibald Willard in 1876 for the hundredth anniversary of the Declaration of Independence, this picture has come to symbolize the spirit of the American Revolution.

Mexico, Venezuela, and most of its other colonies in the New World.

Once the United States became independent, however, it faced the enormous challenge of forging an effective system of government. Though they had co-operated during the war, the individual states were reluctant to accept a centralized authority. Finally, in 1787, delegates from the thirteen former colonies met in Philadelphia and devised a plan for governing the new nation: the Constitution of the United States. The Constitution, and the Bill of Rights that was appended to it, are together a remarkable document. Laying down the principles of government by and for the people, it has endured through more than two centuries of changes that the American founders could never possibly have imagined. To this day the words of its preamble ring with the principles for which so many died in the American Revolution:

> We the people of the United States, in order to form a more perfect Union, establish justice, insure domestic tranquility, provide for the common defense, promote the general welfare, and secure the blessings of liberty to ourselves and our posterity, do ordain and establish this Constitution of the United States of America.

# Chronology

1765—Parliament passes the Stamp Act.

1766—The Stamp Act is repealed.

1767—Parliament passes the Townshend Acts.

March 5, 1770—Five Americans die in the Boston Massacre.

December 16, 1773—Patriots throw 342 chests of tea overboard during the Boston Tea Party.

September 1774—First Continental Congress meets in Philadelphia.

April 19, 1775—First shots fired at Lexington and Concord.

May 1775—Benedict Arnold and Ethan Allen capture Ticonderoga and Crown Point.

June 15, 1775—George Washington is appointed Commander-in-Chief of the Continental Army.

June 17, 1775—British troops drive American forces from Breed's Hill.

September 1775—Richard Montgomery and Benedict Arnold set out to invade Canada.

November 13, 1775—Montgomery captures Montreal.

December 31, 1775—Arnold fails to capture Quebec from the British. Montgomery is killed.

March 17, 1776— General Howe evacuates the British from Boston.

July 4, 1776—Congress approves the Declaration of Independence.

August 27, 1776—British victory in the Battle of Long Island.

December 26, 1776—Washington takes Hessian soldiers by surprise at Trenton.

January 3, 1777—Washington defeats British in the Battle of Princeton.

September 11, 1777—Howe defeats Americans at Brandywine and subsequently captures Philadelphia.

October 4, 1776—Washington is defeated at the Battle of Germantown.

October 17, 1777—Gates' American troops defeat British General Burgoyne at Saratoga.

December 19, 1777—George Washington encamps at Valley Forge.

February 6, 1778—France and America sign treaty of alliance in Paris.

June 28, 1778—The Battle of Monmouth ends in a draw.

July 1778—Indians and Loyalists massacre American settlers in Pennsylvania's Wyoming Valley.

December 29, 1778—British occupy Savannah.

February 23–25, 1779—George Rogers Clark recaptures Fort Vincennes.

May 12, 1780—British take Charleston after a six-week siege.

**August 16, 1780**—Cornwallis defeats Gates at Camden, South Carolina.

**September 1780**—Benedict Arnold turns traitor.

**October 6, 1780**—Overmountain men defeat Ferguson and Loyalists at King's Mountain.

**October 1781**—Siege of Yorktown; Cornwallis surrenders to George Washington on October 19th.

**December 14, 1782**—The British finally leave Charleston.

**September 3, 1783**—Treaty of Paris brings the war to an end.

**September 17, 1787**—Delegates from thirteen states approve the United States Constitution.

# Notes by Chapter

## Chapter 1

1. Richard Wheeler, *Voices of 1776* (New York, Thomas Y. Crowell, 1972), p. 4.
2. *Ibid.*, p. 7.
3. *Ibid.*, p. 7.
4. Henry Steele Commager and Richard B. Morris, *The Spirit of Seventy-six: The Story of the American Revolution as Told by Participants (New York, Bonanza Books/Crown, 1983)*, pp. 73–74.
5. *Ibid.*, p. 75.

## Chapter 2

1. Encyclopedia Britannica, *The Annals of America, Vol. 2, Resistance and Revolution: 1755–1783* (Chicago, London, Encyclopedia Britannica, 1976), p. 150.
2. Richard Middlekauff, *The Glorious Cause: The American Revolution, 1763–1789. (New York, Oxford University Press, 1982)*, p. 193.
3. Benjamin. Quarles. *The Negro in the American Revolution* (Chapel Hill, North Carolina, University of North Carolina Press, 1961), pp. 5–6.
4. Henry Steele Commager and Richard B. Morris, *The Spirit of Seventy-six: The Story of the American Revolution as Told by Participants* (New York, Bonanza Books/Crown, 1983), pp. 5–6.

## Chapter 3

1. Henry Steele Commager and Richard B. Morris, *The Spirit of Seventy-six: The Story of the American Revolution as Told by Participants* (New York, Bonanza Books/Crown, 1983), p. 103.

2. Christopher Hibbert, *Redcoats and Rebels: The American Revolution Through British Eyes* (New York, W. W. Norton, 1990), p. 42.

3. Richard Wheeler, *Voices of 1776* (New York, Thomas Y. Crowell, 1972), p. 40.

4. *Ibid.*, p. 42.

5. A. J. Langguth, *Patriots: The Men Who Started the American Revolution.* (New York, Simon & Schuster, 1988), p. 289.

6. Commager and Morris, p. 153.

7. *Ibid.*, p. 443.

## Chapter 4

1. Joy Day Buel and Richard Buel, Jr., *The Way of Duty: A Woman and Her Family in Revolutionary America* (New York, W. W. Norton, 1984), p. 105.

2. Henry Steele Commager and Richard B. Morris. *The Spirit of Seventy-six: The Story of the American Revolution as told by Participants* (New York, Bonanza Books/Crown, 1983), p. 335.

3. John C. Dann, *The Revolution Remembered: Eyewitness Accounts of the War for Independence* (Chicago, University of Chicago Press, 1980), p. 31.

4. Wallace Brown, *The Good Americans:* Loyalists in

the American Revolution (New York, Morrow, 1969), p. 140.

5. Commager and Morris, p. 579.

6. Elizabeth Evans, *Weathering the Storm: Women of the American Revolution* (New York, Scribners, 1975), p. 97.

7. Commager and Morris, p. 856.

8. Commager and Morris, p. 252.

## Chapter 5

1. Henry Steele Commager and Richard B. Morris. *The Spirit of Seventy-six: The Story of the American Revolution as Told by Participants* (New York, Bonanza Books/Crown, 1983), p. 513.

2. *Ibid.*, p. 602.

3. Richard Wheeler, *Voices of 1776* (New York, Thomas Y. Crowell, 1972), p. 260.

4. *Ibid.*, p. 268.

## Chapter 6

1. Richard Wheeler, *Voices of 1776* (New York, Thomas Y. Crowell, 1972), p. 283.

2. Henry Steele Commager and Richard B. Morris. *The Spirit of Seventy-six: The Story of the American Revolution as Told by Participants.* (New York, Bonanza Books/Crown, 1983), p. 1042.

3. Papers at the Illinois State Historical Museum, Springfield, Illinois.

4. Commager and Morris, p. 969.

5. Christopher Hibbert, *Redcoats and Rebels: The*

*American Revolution Through British Eyes* (New York, W. W. Norton, 1990), p. 277.

6. *Ibid.*, p. 283.

7. John C. Dann, *The Revolution Remembered: Eyewitness Accounts of the War for Independence* (Chicago, University of Chicago Press, 1980), p. 244.

8. *Ibid.*, p. 245.

9. Theodore Thayer, *Yorktown: Campaign of Strategic Options* (Philadelphia, Lippincott, 1975), p. 59.

# Further Reading

Bruce Bliven, *The American Revolution*. New York: Random House, 1958.

Alden R. Carter, *At the Forge of Liberty*. New York: Franklin Watts, Inc., 1988.

Alice Dalgliesh, *The Fourth of July Story*. New York: Macmillan, 1956.

Albert Marrin, *The War for Independence: The Story of the American Revolution*. New York: Macmillan, 1988.

Milton Meltzer, *The American Revolutionaries: A History in Their Own Words, 1750–1800*. New York: Thomas Y. Crowell, 1987.

Richard B. Morris, *The American Revolution*. Lerner, 1985.

R. Conrad Stein, *The Story of Lexington and Concord*. Childrens Press, 1983.

# Index

## About the Author

Deborah Kent grew up in Little Falls, New Jersey. She received a B.A. from Oberlin College in Oberlin, Ohio, and a Master's Degree from Smith College School for Social Work. After four years as a social worker at the University Settlement House on New York City's Lower East Side, she decided to try her hand at writing. She moved to San Miguel de Allende, a Mexican town with a large community of writers and artists. Her first novel, *Belonging*, appeared in 1978.

Ms. Kent is the author of more than a dozen young-adult novels, as well as many nonfiction books for children. She lives in Chicago with her husband, children's-book author R. Conrad Stein, and their daughter Janna.